THE MOMENTS OF LIFE

SWATHISENDIL

I Dedicate this book 'The Moments of Life' to my very supportive mom S. Pramila and father R. Sendilkumaran. Secondly to Lord Shiva who is guiding me through the hard times and to the almighty and goddesses of this universe. I'm honor bound to dedicate it to all my professors and friends. I have to thank all my relatives who are the pillars of my life.

Contents

Contents

Preface

This book is meant for the people who wishes to know the journey between life and death. The rise and the fall are balances of life which makes the life more interesting. This book describes the best and the worst too. But in the end it tells about how to look optimism in pessimism to this pessimistic world.

Acknowledgements

I hereby feel responsible to acknowledge my professors. Raji ma'am, Eshwari ma'am and Bavya ma'am all these three professors of mine have a great part in finding my talents and bringing it out.

1. Poetry Forever

Poetry touched every cells of me,
Ink flows as blood in my veins,
She has the magic,
In bringing my dead soul alive,
Being a poet is a gift,
It gifts the absolute love and joy,
The life of poet is a delight,
Everything becomes poetical in their life,
In every emotion hand searches for the pen,
Poetry fills my cup of insight,
With ingredients such as richness and delicacy,
I'm unsure of the reason for what I fell in love,
With you,
But, it is my destiny to meet you and fall in love,
I accept you with grace and smile.
Each moment when I write you,
I feel that I'm blessed by God of Knowledge.
All the muses of poetry,
I invoke you,
To guide me through each lines and words,
It is you, who is going to make me alive,
Even after the expiry of my body,

Keep breathing so will I.

2. Shiva: The Legend

Mahadev, Shiva, Neelkanth…
His identity reveals his great stature!
Trishul, his destructive weapon,
Is also great as his identity!
Uttering his name as Mantra,
Brings eternal energy in lives!
He being obsessed with dusk, sunset,
Gifts the elixir of optimism in pessimism!
Ever thankful to the holiest Kailash,
For presenting him to the Earth!
His magnificent body has no hint of fear,
For he wears serpent as an ornament!
His emotions are synonym of extremity,
The emotions love, anger, and dance are lively,
Because of him, the lord Shiva!
Love of Shiva towards his Parvati,
Reflects pure and real love!
Anger or wrath of Shiva is the end,
The greatest threat for an evil thinker!
Dance of Shiva is the dance of universe,
It is the utmost pleasure one can witness!
Admiring his abilities, deeds, virtues,

Stops one from committing treason!
Rusted, wounded soul and heart,
Heals by his presence and love!
Worshipping him and driving his energy into us,
Pushes us to do the impossibles!
His presence can make an atheist,
Believe in God, Miracles and Wonders!
Feeling him by the heart,
Is the greatest gift and pleasure of one!
The mantra 'Shiva',
Is the birth of hope, faith and optimism!
There's secret elixir in 'Shiva',
For he's celebrated, cherished and loved!

3. Gods

Gods are plenty, in this earth,
Each believe to whom they adhere to,
Few might say, Krishna is the best God,
There are people, who assert Allah is everything,
Some might say, Christ is God of Gods,
But, there's none like that,
Every God is equal and same,
We for our convenience, categorize Gods,
By giving different identities, various forms,
Sayings of all the Gods are similar,
They teach us to do good, not evil,
God and Goddess say plenty of goods,
But, are we accepting and following it?
We love partition than unity,
None of the sacred texts, that exists,
Like Bhagavad Gita, Bible, Quran…,
Tells us to kill each other,
In the name of the Gods,
We fulfill our greed, lust and desire,
Beliefs and superstitious beliefs are confused,
Murdering the little child for wealth,
It is the cruelest superstitious belief,

Praying for the guidance in the task,
It is the positive belief on the God,
That he's there to guide us,
Almighty is present everywhere in universe,
They are the parents of galaxy,
None can cheat them and flee,
Having belief in yourself and God,
Gives one the strength to finish challenges,
The Gods want us to live in serenity,
But, we destroy the peace ourselves,
In pointless battles, fights, bloodsheds.

4. Birth

Little buds bloom,

When warm sun caress her,

A new flower is born.

Rising from ashes,

Without fear, hesitation, doubtfulness,

Phoenix begot mastery.

Tides crawling,

To lick the salt in the shore,

A new tide is born in the lap of sea.

Rising between clouds, mountain passes and peaks,

With sheer beauty and glowing warmth,

Sun spreads birth of dawn and faith.

Little sapling,

Trying her best to live her life,

She gives stern confidence to the globe.

Glowing light from little piece of thread,

With sheer radiance, firmness,

Lamp brings in birth of desire.

Stirring the mind,

Bringing out the best of all decisions,

A new idea breaks all the problems.

Raging pulse from inside,

With new feelings, emotions,
Love begins to grow in little heart.
Finding our right path,
Beginning to tread in it despite hurdles,
Passion never sees the pessimistic side.
Every micro thing that exists,
In this universe,
Has a birth that has meaning and destiny.
A birth that we all have,
It is a treasure of all,
A human birth is that treasure.
As humans,
We're blessed with goodness and evilness,
We're shown both love and hatred,
We're gifted with success and failure,
We're given pain and healings.
The decision is on us,
How we desire to take on life.
Being unique, precise and one in a million,
Requires a birth but not an ordinary birth,
A birth that is rare,
Make you birth the rarest!

5. Life

Life is a gift,
All gift boxes haven't same gifts,
Each gift box is unique by its content.
Our life is a gift of valuables.
Been born as human is a gift of delight.
Each day,
Each day,
God sends us a gift box,
Some open it with dare,
They succeed in their lives.
Many fear opening it,
Thus they lose their opportunities.
Very few accept the gift boxes,
That has sorrows and happiness.
People neglect box of sorrows,
Since, they don't want to know the truth.
Life is a gift of sea.
The tides taste the shore,
And it goes back to swallow itself.
Likewise the life has its rise,
And the same has a fall.
Life is a gift of elements.

Some threatening moments of life,
Are to be fired and burnt alive,
That shows the beauty of fearless life.
Some moments are to be consoled,
Like pouring icy water over burning house,
That makes us to have deserving bonds beside.
Some incidents should be blown,
Like the invisible air,
That helps us in overcoming obstacles.
Fulfillment in life happens,
At the moment when our passion turns true,
That has been our dream for years.
Every day of our life,
Is ours, so it should be our own design,
That makes us to have novelty.
Life is a gift of emotions,
That makes us as a human being,
It distinguishes us from five sense creatures.
To enjoy it at present,
And holding the past as memories,
For later days that is yet to come.
Life is a gift of Gods,
When used wisely, they bless us with more.
Live your life as it is gifted.

6. Passion

Passion is the soul,
That keeps the body alive.
Once our passion is discovered,
Passion never wavers.
Yet, anything will be ignored,
Just for the sake of Passion.
Passion lies in the breath of heart.
Enforced passion,
Neither is soulful nor alive.
The bud of enforced passion,
Never in ages turns to a blooming flower.
From the mind of love and willingness,
A passion should be born.
Such passion born from love and commitment,
Will never fail and die,
Tons of obstacles may fled in,
A path full of thorns might be the hurdle,
But obstacles and hurdles,
Will be blown like ashes of dust,
It blooms like the rarest flower,
That never dries even in drought.
A passion blooms with merriness,

With all the failures and disgust,
To the flower of success,
It never turns barren,
Instead it burst out as seeds,
That falls in the soil,
To give life to many young buds,
As a lighthouse,
Guides the ships to the shore,
The seeds give life to many,
A passion is that light of the lamp,
Where it keeps glowing,
Without being altered.
It's not like wild fire in the forest,
That keeps fuming one day,
But calms in couple of days.
Passion is a path of constancy,
Where the destiny is fixed,
But the hard path is never minded.
Hold the passion,
As you hold your breath,
Fight for your passion,
As you fight for your life,
Follow passion with heart and mind,
To make your passion,
A reality,
That makes you meaningful.

7. Pen

A bond lives between me and my pen,
Like, I share with my parents, friends.
I wish not to address my pen as 'it',
Instead I wish to refer my pen as 'She'.
At times when I pick her up,
I don't let her down for hours,
I keep draining her energy,
Her blood keeps flowing,
Throughout the day and night,
She's the one, who knows all my secrets,
Though she feels weary,
She never fails to bring me,
The dawn of success,
And a broad smile on my lips,
She changes my soulful thoughts to words,
She is never going to rust,
She knows my best and the worst,
She has seen all my phases,
Bright smiles, teary eyes,
Anger, broken me, agony and all,
What would've I done?
If you haven't fallen between my fingers,

My fingers would have been useless,
My pen and I would feel purposeful,
If we were able to bring change,
In the life of a single person,
From the darkness to the light,
This bond will last forever,
And none can destroy this bond.

8. Apology

Seeking apology from the heart,
Heals the wound, scar,
I have squeezed your life and soul,
Despite humanity, I do it at all times,
But you make my life what it is!
You endure my pain, to bring my thoughts alive,
If not you, I would've been traumatized,
Vampires would've sucked my blood,
Lord of death would've taken me off,
Tsunami waves could've thrown me,
Meteor shower would have burnt me alive,
To flee from these traps,
I never bothered your agony,
I apologize for my blunders,
For hurting you, tormenting you,
I've to seek forgiveness,
From the persons,
Those who carries me whenever I fall,
Dark blood from the wounds,
Kept flowing in your body,
Making you injured heavily,
I seek apologies from you for bruising you,

To both pen, pages,
I keep seeking the apology,
Forever, till I breathe my last,
Hope this bond,
Continues in all my upcoming birth,
And I seek your forgiveness,
For the births, till I enter,
Into my final salvation!

9. Penning Poetry

Sitting in the hard rock,
Merging legs in the icy pond,
Wild trees creating bizarre hymns,
Birds murmuring among themselves,
White bright moon reflecting in waters,
Is the feast for eyes!
The most delightful moment,
That a soul yearns for,
Is to witness,
Happy tears of mountain in its cheek,
As tears rolls from the eyes, in the cheeks.
Waters giggling when reaching down,
Is the special gift from nature!
Inhaling such a pleasure,
Captivating the moment as if it is mine,
I hurriedly grabbed a pen and a paper,
To put the pleasure in words,
I lost myself in nature's bliss.
Suddenly my ears noted,
A strange buzz,
Sshhh, sshhh,
It persisted.

Is it a serpent?
My inner voice questioned my brain,
The serpent it is.
Not one, but two!
And, to my shocking surprise,
They are king of serpents,
They're king Cobras.
Some twenty meters of their body,
Kept circling beside me,
Initially I thought I'm going to die,
And my breathing turned to a whisper,
I'm completely wronged,
Their movements aren't threatening,
The proud heads of Cobras,
Stood upright in front of me,
As a child leans forward,
To hear tales and fables from mother,
Those cobras leant forward,
To hear something from me,
I understood they need a companion.
Shelving all my fears away,
I began speaking with them,
The cobras felt immense joy,
Bowed their proud heads,
As a token of friendship,
The two cobras put a show for me,
Their movements are lovely,

The bond,
Of Cobras and Me,
I wish to cherish and preserve it for life,
They became my friends,
They followed me, wherever I went.
The kings offered me,
A warm protection,
Which no one could offer!
When writing verses,
I realize that I'm destined to,
So I wish to keep penning poetries,
As long as my fingers could hold the pen,
And some thoughts circle in my mind.

10. English

English, though you're a foreigner,
You're now my soul, heart throb and what not?
You entered my life as a mariner,
Who parked my life in best port!
My dear English, though you're a colonizer,
I can't stand against you,
I fell in love with your accent,
You broke my thoughts of being inferior,
Through which you implied a purpose of my life.
English, though you're a destroyer,
Of the millions of lives,
You have sown the seeds of trillion flowers,
You're good at life preserver,
I get immense love by your presence in my life.
My poetry, my words falls short,
Each day I wish to relish myself in your presence,
What not? What not? What not?
Without you,
My garden would have been without a flower.
In your absence,
Like a rootless tree my life would have been,
Like a body without a soul.

11. Literature

The best choice, that I ever made,
It is choosing you over science, technology.
You filled my life with different shades.
Poetries, fictions, short stories, plays,
Non-fictions, proses, essays,
Whatever forms you take,
You are very literature to me,
And I love you,
As long as my memory could hold you,
As poetry, you unveiled real beauty of the world,
As fiction, you presented an imaginary life,
As short story, you emphasized moral,
As play, you said we all are artists,
As prose, you educate readers,
As essay, you tune the wiser academicians,
As literature, you made me feel complete.
Viewing life, in your lens,
Is like looking an object through coolers,
It's such precise and cool.
The little nuances are precisely revealed.
Literature is delight,
Delight of wisdom, optimism and intelligence,

Drenching in such delight,
Gifts a chance to understand life better.
Shakespeare's stunning sonnets, pressing plays,
Wordsworth's realistic romantic verses,
Chaucer's captivating Canterbury Tales,
Queen Elizabeth's Golden rule of British Dynasty,
Bacon's benefitting essays,
Spenser's scintillating poems, proses,
University wits uplifting literature in unique way,
Milton, Dryden and pope exhibiting their own mantle,
Woolf's wild truthful writing,
Atwood aspiring youth through her Survival,
Tagore being a gift to Indian literature,
Sarojini Naidu's daring poetries,
Amish Tripathi's modernized myths,
Are all is a treasure of literature.
Different ages, different epochs, may arise,
But, Culture, tradition, language travels through literature,
From one generation to the another,
Literature is diversity, where,
Literature has the undeniable beginning,
But runs without an end.
Literature flourishes each day.
Being a little drop of the ocean,
It is the best of it!

12. Books

Choosing the book,
It is destined for a person,
It is neither through the gist,
Nor the attractive covers.
It is the bond that exists,
Between a person and the book!
That bond tempts us to pick the book,
With love, hope and affection,
Dwelling into the treasure,
To experience the new adventure,
To inherit the values of life,
To get influenced by characters,
To live life as we desire.
Great books steers us crazy,
Though hundreds of pages,
It won't allow us to let it down,
But keep going for days and nights!
A Rare book drives us insane,
Tears shed in characters is ours,
Their smile is our smile,
And their suffering is our own!
Acknowledgement is the best part of the book,

For it recognizes the peers,
Who stood by the author's hard times!
It's the heart melting moment,
Winning or losing doesn't matter.
Every author,
Puts their heart into the books,
Day and night they work with love,
Weariness isn't a matter for them,
There's no author in this world,
Where they cook something,
And serves it to the readers!
They delicately choose,
The thing that's needed to be scripted,
Thing that's wanted to be presented,
They decide it with care and concern.
All books aren't same,
Each book is special by its own features,
Every book deserves to be read,
Some books tempts us,
To read again and again,
For several times, for its uniqueness!
Experiencing the adventure of reading books,
Smelling the insane essence of book,
Enjoying each lines,
Living among the characters,
Imagining the scenic beauties,
Are the pleasures of reading books!

Each one is gifted with such pleasures,
Few enjoy the deepest,
Some cherish it with love,
Countable people take it to life.

13. India

India is a land of emotions,
When uttering the name 'India',
Invisible ecstasy rages in the heart,
India's pride lies in duties, trust, responsibilities,
A word said is said,
No one dares to break the promises,
From Jammu Kashmir to Kanyakumari,
Several heritage, customs, traditions,
Flourish in diversity with valor.
Various states, different cities, unique capitals,
Recites the grandeur of India,
Indian soil has historical bloodsheds,
Of our great warriors and contemporary soldiers,
Our liberty they gifted us is by striving hard,
They have been tormented in prison,
Their suffering ends only in the death,
But the brave hearts never withered,
They kept fighting,
Till the last drop of blood oozed out,
Such hard is our sweet liberty.
Our India never considers anyone as foes,
But few consider us as rivalries,

Their notion draws a line between,
Spiritual, divine waters touching all the corners,
Shows the mammoth creation of the God,
India is rightfully named after Mother, 'Mother India',
How beautiful the term 'Mother India' is!
It is the deserving recognition for Mothers of India,
India turns paradise on the earth,
When women feel secure,
Then India will be the golden bowl of galaxy.
The pledge that's taken,
'All Indians are my brothers and sisters',
It is true in reality.
Differences separate us, but we're united,
By our bonds,
That is through love, affection, bliss.
India is God of help,
When it comes to crisis and need,
India never fails to lend helping hands,
Irrespective of relationship,
Sending medical aids, food supplies,
India stands unbeaten.
India's actions might create fury in hatred's heart,
But the haters made to do so.
Gradually, India is turning to be Independent,
For which, Indians should be pride of themselves.
A land dwelled deep in miracles, is India.
Miracles of ancestry, history, treasures, successful people,

Has a synonym called India!
Every inch of India,
It is filled with cultural values.
India will never fail,
Until the last Indian soul exists,
We will bring glory to our India together.
My love for India will never wither,
My soul is duty bound to love India.
Love India as you love yourself,
India will love you back,
Thousand and lakh of times!
Embrace India,
As you embrace your mother,
India nurses you as a loving mother,
India is a mother for our mother,
My pride lies in,
Bringing glory to our mother,
What's your pride?

14. Home

The doors that is always welcoming,
Walls carrying the emotions than bricks,
Objects eavesdropping conversations,
Lovely talks, heated commotions…,
Hangers displaying memories,
Special moments hanging in iron nails,
Living rooms shifting to parliaments every day,
Showcases showing the achievements of family,
Bookshelves holding the favorite collections,
Lovely miniatures residing in a corner,
Televisions that keep crying in the center,
Curtains making the partitions,
Doors locking secret documents behind,
Dining room that's never used,
Pooja room being the soul of home,
Prayers welcoming all the goodness inside,
Kitchen taking the pride of heart of home,
Greens, vegetables, spices making the home healthy,
Study corner that's visited often,
Writing more than reading in the study corner,
Polished swings getting the special attention,
Wardrobes hanging lovely outfits,

Mirrors reflecting the unity of the family,
Rooms holding tons of secrets,
Clocks tickling here and there,
Store room suffocating with lot of stuffs,
Staircases pushing us forward,
Garden grooming freshness in life,
Plants speaking to us in secret languages,
People showing love and care,
All these lively things make a home as a home,
Home embraces us all the times,
She never pulls us off,
The palaces, bungalows can't offer peace,
But the home can, and so it is called.
Home is where life takes a meaning,
Home has a lot to say,
More than it actually tells people.

15. Unity

Scattered around globe,
States may part us,
Districts may differentiate us,
By birth we may be divided,
The religions slices our bonds,
Class status might leave us separated,
Languages may be a partition,
Caste systems can be a barrier,
We have our endless battles,
For caste, community, state…,
The battles happen every day,
But,
One emotion, one word, one feeling,
Crushes the partition, differences, discriminations, pessimism,
And unites us together as the glue,
That single mantra is 'INDIA'.
Being an Indian,
No single Indian will ever watch,
Their mother getting insulted, ill-mouthed,
The rage and fury of the Indians,
Have the power to bury them alive,
And the scar lasts forever,

For births to come,
India unites billions of Indians together!

16. Warriors

While others shed sweat,
For their nation's growth,
Warriors shed blood as their sweat,
For the nation they love,
They carry in their heart, breath and mind.
Their service to the homeland,
Is an indisputable service!
Parting away from blood relations,
Being unable to see them for months,
It's difficult even for the lion hearts.
Physically, mentally it needs efforts.
Indian warriors stand ahead among all,
The bravery of our people,
Invites fear in the heart and eyes of foes,
They care about their life second,
Since, they aim to protect the nation.
Unstable is warrior's life,
They need to be a spy agent,
Change their identity to find something,
Bear the killing snow,
Be under the boiling sun,
To keep an eagle eye,

In the borders of our pride nation,
Their life is doubtful,
Army people and warriors,
Need to be worshipped and respected,
For they are the living Gods,
Who stand between the death and life!
They take bullets for us,
They lose their life,
They leave back all the personal desires,
They needn't do these things,
Yet they do it with love,
Turning themselves as MARTYRS!
As I'm writing this verse,
In the borders of Jammu and Kashmir,
My brother or sister,
Would've been dead or injured…
But, their death is unnoticed.
Honoring the warrior after the death,
By presenting a posthumous award,
It is just a bit of recognition,
If a single soldier dies in the border,
That day is loss for the nation,
The soldiers' death is not an ordinary death,
They voluntarily seek death wish.
If not warriors, remember,
Unimaginable is peaceful life and day.
Indians should carry them in heart,

Their bravery, skills and love for the nation,
And follow them in their path.
To be a threat to the nation,
That wishes to ruin our integrity and peace.
Let us all be warriors,
To fight for our nation,
To fight for our mother's safety,
Till we breathe our very last.
A salute and bow to the Indian warriors.

17. Mother

A true selfless being of this selfish society,
It is God, who creates us,
But, it is a mother who gives life to us,
If there's love that never comes down,
It's the mother's love to the child,
She's an angel without wings of magic,
Be it daughter or son,
She knows how to love them,
She knows how to protect them,
She educates the life lessons to the child,
Mother's upbringing of a child,
It is a blessed one,
None of the curses brings harm for the child,
For a mother a child is always a child,
Though the child turns sixty,
She won't decrease the love,
Instead as days passes by,
She pours more and more love on them.
A girl when she discovers,
Her pregnancy, her happiness knew no bound,
She experiences the joy of ecstasy.
Being or to be mother,

Adds extra beauty to her,
For ten months,
She endures each and every agony,
For the little bud to blossom on the fine day,
Enduring the labor pain,
For a woman is like,
Entering the gates of hell being alive,
Relationship that never withers,
It is of a mother and a child.
The pain that she endures,
Tears that rolls down her cheeks,
Turns as the brightest smile of her life,
More than a father,
It is a mother,
Where she can understand the child's emotions,
That is unsaid and uttered!
A mother's instinct never wrongs,
She senses the child's problems,
Though the child and mother are apart,
Mother, indeed,
It's a universal feeling and emotion,
That's common around the globe.
A mother though she is hurt by her child,
She never curses her child,
And it's only the heart of mother.
Respecting, caring and loving a mother,
Is the best way to pay back your deeds of debt!

A mother's blessing,
Takes you to the heights,
Which you haven't imagined in your life,
Seek your mother's blessings,
With duty, love and respect,
To feel the optimism and miracle,
Each day wonders knock your life!

18. Father

The safest spot in the earth,
For a child,
It is the father's shoulder and arms.
A girl child is father's greatest love,
When he carries her in his hands,
His tears break unconsciously,
And his hard and rough cheeks,
Turns soft by tears soaking in it,
His smile is a gift by God,
When she grows, she's protected in his heart.
For a girl, the real joy of ecstasy,
It is holding her father's hand,
And taking up the challenges of life,
Her joy lies in taking a nap in his lap.
Riding in bike hugging her daddy,
To the another galaxy,
It is always her first priority.
But, a girl and a father is cursed,
By this corrupted society.
Until her age allows her,
She can hold her daddy,
As much as she needs,

Once she becomes a girl,
Where she begins her menstrual cycle,
She has to consider her daddy as a stranger,
Who did impossible tasks and did anything,
Just to make her smile.
This hasn't changed from the ancient times,
And even in this modern world.
Girl child keeps growing,
Just to be the reflection of her father.
Her growing up,
Increases the distances between them.
Lovely little nuances,
That exists between father and daughter,
Gets to happen hardly,
But, the girl has to live,
With the memories that she has,
That gifts the everlasting love.
A father's son grows,
To be a man of righteous character,
He has all the morals and values,
Absorbed from his father,
Respecting woman he knows the best,
He has no evil deeds in him.
A father gets to believe his son,
For he has grown under his shadow,
Beyond these,
A father is the iconic hero of his son,

Daddy is the first love of his daughter.
A father is second selfless creature.
He passes the best, not the worst.
He inherits all the worst things,
That is going to fall on his children.
As you grow up,
Give some rest to your father,
As he is weary of running.
Daddy's girl and father's son,
It is one among the best bonds,
That is ever lively and pleasing.

19. Professor

Melting their life each day,
As a melting candle,
Igniting wisdom in the mind and heart,
Professors never deny their duty.
Creative creators of the society,
Are the professors who live in temple!
They create all the professionals,
Yet they are behind the curtains,
Unspoken is their valor.
It's a blessing of a God,
For a student,
To get a great professor,
Mean not to say,
Some professors are bad.
Profession of professors,
It is the best one but hardly spoken of.
Each professor is God,
For they pass the sound wisdom,
Values and morals that shapes the students,
Molding their disciples,
Making them rich by the character,
Creating the best society,

Without the magic stick they do all.
Such virtuous deeds of a professor,
Are unsung and unveiled in society,
That's pathetic and regretful.
It's not the actor, actress,
In televisions and cinemas,
Where they flaunt their beauty and skills,
Can be called as icons,
It's the teachers and professors,
Where they enrich the palace of wisdom,
Are the real icons of the universe!
Living Gods, Goddess are the Professors,
A student who earns,
The blessing of a professor,
She gets to reach her destiny.
The blunders that the students make,
The professors never fail to correct it.
In a student's life,
A great teacher,
Exceeds beyond the boundaries,
To sow the seeds of wisdom,
To inspire the soil,
To behold rarest fruit or flower,
That brings the speck of light in their disciple.
History never lies or exaggerates,
Great men are inspired by Great Teachers,
Great teachers change the fate of destiny,

They can make a beautiful sculpture,
Out of barren land that is useless.
As students,
The primary duty,
Is to worship our professors,
Each passing day,
Till our own death!

20. Friendship

Special, elixir, lively, pleasant…
All make friendship deliciously dined dessert,
When life is hard, it brings honey,
When sick, it heals with medicine,
When hunger, it feeds food,
When lonely, it turns as a companion.
Gorgeous, lovely, guiding, trustworthy…
All make friendship a unique bond.
When needed, friend turns as a mother,
When sought righteous protection, she turns as a father,
When fighting, she resembles siblings fight,
When advising for hours, she resembles nanny,
All in all,
Friendship remains unsuspicious, undoubted,
It stays firm in thick and thin,
Such is the beauty of friendship,
Feel the elixir of friendship,
By having friends to stand with you!
Friendships are always crazy,
Since everything happens insanely,
Between the beautiful bonds!

21. College Diary

A new life,
A new beginning,
Exploring the hidden talents,
Change of thoughts, behaviorism,
Realizing our responsibility,
Making new friends,
Learning for life than marks,
Getting inspired by the professors,
Participating in all events,
Winning and losing matters least,
Dias still holding my footprints,
Last bench being my favorite,
Trees knowing our stories,
Having friends in all departments,
Getting the overall championship,
Enrolling in a play,
Practicing a lot for it,
Understanding each other a lot more,
Conferences helping us to socialize,
Compering scripts changing till the last,
Attending events in various colleges,
Winning in state level,

It is the special feel,
Award ceremony and semesters falling close,
Going some hundred miles away,
Collecting the award and returning back,
Assembly week turning interesting,
Industrial visit turning to be the best part,
Having so much fun on the way,
Everything went fine,
Until the deadliest of plagues hit the globe,
Offline classes getting canceled for months,
Missing the farewell, food fest, tour,
It is the hell a kind of feeling,
Having no ideas of online classes,
But, starting to learn the techniques,
Online attendance being the headache,
Online exams increasing the anxiety,
But, I had the best lecturers,
Finishing graduation with some emptiness,
Entering into masters with expectations,
Having some new friends,
Online classes taking few months of masters,
Being appointed as the class representative,
Collecting data, records, information every day,
Winning the best student award,
Hearing praises from my favorite ma'am,
It is the best moment of all,
The millions of dollars can't buy the happiness,

THE MOMENTS OF LIFE

The koffee house club being mine,
Never leaving a single competition,
Being the treasurer of the club,
Delivering the chief guest introduction,
Valediction day being mine,
Receiving prizes one after another,
Visiting the far away college,
Leaving the examination behind,
Participating in a speech competition,
Winning district third,
Realizing that I'm going to get award,
That too from honorable CM,
Knowing that I'm doing justice,
Praises flooding in my chats, calls,
My favorite ma'am announcing my success,
It is the moment that I waited for,
Meeting the honorable chief minister,
Getting my award,
Again love and praises pouring in my way,
Choosing the project title that is destined,
Successfully completing it on time,
Viva voce arriving near,
Presenting the project as dreamt of,
Operating the system for my friends,
Each and every day being the best,
Being unable to bid farewell,
The hardest thing is to part with friends, professors,

All the memories makes the college days,
As the sweetest one in life!

22. Women

Waking before dawn, finishing chores,
Preparing Coffee, Tea, Horlicks, Milk,
Serving it with affection,
Yet longing for a peaceful morning,
Chopping vegetables, pouring banter in platters,
Dining protein rich foods,
Dressing up kids for school,
Ironing suits for husband for his work,
Hurrying herself for her job,
Doing all the works in workspace,
Finishing the work quickly,
Riding back home, to be there before kids,
Preparing nutritious diets for the family,
Again serving her children,
Teaching her children,
Helping them to finish their assignments,
Preparing Coffee, Tea, Horlicks, Milk,
Finishing dinner duties,
Serving in platters, like the waitress in restaurant,
Taking what's left and remaining,
Gaining all the goodness for the family,
Doing all the things to upgrade the family,

Family, family, family,
Does anyone in the family care for her?
No, seriously not, hardly it happens,
Caring, loving, protecting is her duty to her family,
Expecting the same from her family,
It is an offense,
For which she can be imprisoned,
In the walls of the home prison,
Change should start from a family,
Where all woman is loved, cared, respected,
By her husband, children and in-laws,
Only then a home can stay peaceful.
Women are prospering too,
In the fields that we haven't prospered,
So it's the time to take our roles!
Let's flourish together!

23. Fall of a Woman

'She is weaker, he is stronger',
The phrase is heard everywhere.
It is a blunder of statement.
She isn't weaker,
She carrying the fetus in womb,
She undergoes all the pain in the world,
In the period of ten months,
And she delivers her baby,
Bearing all kinds of agony,
But she does it with grace.
She isn't fragile,
Period cramps buries her alive,
For a week every month,
She has to endure the killing pain,
Daringly she endures it.
She handles her periods and work,
Simultaneously, that shows her strength.
She isn't weaker.
Yet the society till claims her to be weak, fragile, distraught…
When she gives birth to a child,
She has to sacrifice her career, desire…
For the sake of upbringing the child,

She has to raise the child,
With all the goodness, morals and virtues,
As if she is the only responsible person,
For the child, she has to do everything,
As a father, he should earn money for family,
Is that the only role of the father?
If he is considered to be stronger,
Let he carry the baby,
Let he undergo the period cramps,
A day of such will be the hell,
Then, in what terms,
The society terms him as stronger,
A woman shouldn't be ferocious, scream or fight,
If she did so, she's not an ideal woman.
At times, society fails to recognize,
That she has own heart,
And that heart has dreams, passions, goals,
But those things aren't valued,
A woman is made to fall in her life,
Every day, every minute,
But the society doesn't know,
That She is a like a Phoenix,
Where she rises from her fall,
A woman is stronger,
Than a man,
In all the means,
She has her own swag to give comeback,

Even though she has fallen infinite times,
Stronger, stronger and stronger!

24. Molestation

Stains that never vanish,
Safety of the soul of mankind,
Is like a law scripted in air,
It flies every day.
The disgusting act of man,
Lowers the standards of the society,
Victim being victimized infinite times,
It is the cruelest thing against woman,
The culprit flies off from the case.
Woman's family facing continuous insults,
For the crimes that they haven't done,
It's like stabbing someone who's dead,
Brutally for pleasure of the blood,
Is this the society that I'm living in?
I feel threatened and insecure.
"Justice for… justice for…
How many justices…
But so far, are the justices served?
Hardly the justice is ignored.
This isn't democracy, liberty, bliss,
It's cruel, betrayal, mole of society.
Woman's life turns hell,

The pain and scar haunts her for ages,
Few overcome it,
Several women remain in dark for life,
The words by society tear the heart,
Than the physical pain of women,
That she underwent during molestation.
Is this the land of peace?
NO.
Land that is addressed after 'Mother',
Ah, mother itself gets molested,
Land that's closely acquainted with daughters,
Oh, some cruel fathers impregnating their daughters.
But, I'm blessed,
My father and men in my family,
Are the purest diamonds on the earth!
My men knew to protect the,
They respect and support us,
Because of the men of my family,
I fly with the wings to the heights,
The land with such pure diamonds,
Are also corrupted with needless stones,
A women's pain and her sufferings,
Gives a guilty heart,
The life that haunts him forever,
That he will have till the last day of his life.

25. Love

Love, the stream that never runs dry,
It's like the lovely flowers,
Bloomed in the tree of Paradise,
It is as pure as the rain drops,
That woos the ground,
Music and hymns of love,
It is the best melody and harmony.
Love is the only hand that evaporates,
The tears that runs in cheeks,
The love soaked me in drenches,
Love isn't studious but emotional.
Conditional love never lasts forever,
Love is unconditional,
It never wavers in the strong wind,
Yet, the trust will be the reason,
That holds the root of love stronger.
Love is turning to lust and desire,
That turns beautiful love to ugly emotion,
Such love born out of lust,
It is not love at all.
Love has a magic spell,
That turns a dry leaf into green one,

That spell brings into the life,
The charisma that is lively.
True love has in it,
Both giving and taking,
A love like that will have cognition,
That makes itself unique.
Real love in the heart,
Reflects in the eyes,
That cannot be hidden or covered,
Like the beauty of the sun,
That is reflected in the sheer waters of sea,
Both sun and sea glows in radiance.
Love flourishes in this world,
Until the humanity is alive,
A love will never put stops,
To acquire the dream and passion of each,
Such love has not dawned in my life,
But the dawn may appear sooner than I think,
Neither I'm interested, nor am I uninterested,
But between this somewhere,
Is that love? Maybe…

26. Marriage

Destined in heaven they say,
The two hearts making itself one,
To be one forever till death,
Marriage brings in the ecstatic moment,
The joy, pleasure, love all flood together,
Some marriages bloom from love,
And few love stories emerge after marriage,
Both have love and joy in it.
The day of marriage brings all the smiles,
As blessings from the dearest ones,
Gifts bliss for bride and groom.
It is not only uniting hearts but,
Two culture, two families bonding together,
Walking down the aisle in the chamber,
Glowing bride in bridal attire,
Blushing by the side of her cheeks and eyes,
Making her gorgeous than ever seen.
Awaiting groom for his bride with all charm,
Witnessing his bride walking down the aisle,
Shedding a tear in the corner of his eye,
Holding the hands firmly,
Climbing the auspicious dais together,

Making and Promising vows to each other.
Taking blessings from Lord Agni, Goddess Lakshmi,
Seeking blessings of Gods and Goddess,
Capturing each moment of their best day,
Inviting all angels and muses through recitation of hymns,
Blessing the couple in all means,
Seeking ancestors blessings for fulfillment,
Tying three knots for beautiful bond to last forever,
Sharing life with all the love,
Picking lovely fights,
Praising each other for no reasons,
Complementing each other for the best,
Understanding each other for the better life,
Driving in endless road of infinite joy,
Saying truth than mere flattery,
Marrying with blessings and love,
Living life as they desire for themselves,
Sailing together till the end in same ship,
Winning the lives together,
Marriage brings sweetness in life.

27. Experiences

Experience is at times gleeful, gloomy.
Gleeful in lens of experiencing wonders, achievements,
Gloomy when facing terrible situations,
Experiencing both is a boon of gift by God.
It prepares us to lead a healthy life.
Experience teaches management and art,
Management brings perfection in our lives,
Art makes us creative and to see life beyond boundary lines,
Experiencing both is a boon of gift by God.
It drives us in the lane that's filled with challenges,
To achieve the task that he desires us to achieve.
Experiences are never a trash,
That goes to the bin,
But it's a treasure of life,
That brings in the different perspectives.
Experiences are never taught,
By parents, professors or universities,
But, it's a self-learning on life,
That grooms us from the inside,
Each little experience is a treasure,
That is to be experienced.
Experience every little thing,

That creates the best version of yours,
Every day!

28. Treading by River

Steering the steering wheel,
To the destination that heals me,
It is the thing that I love to do, very often.
Freshness that embrace me,
As I open the door,
It is the love of nature that flourishes.
As I walk in bare legs,
They leave footprints in the gentle land,
Gush of air gently clashing in my cheeks,
With love and sweetness,
That makes my cheeks red,
Puff of my hair popping out,
Welcoming brooks just few steps away,
As nearing her she churns in my ears,
Dedicating the melody to the visitor,
Catamaran sails as the wind pushes it,
A fisherman prays to her sea mother,
For giving him a fair chance,
He throws his nets in the belly of sea,
Cluster of fishes takes him by surprise,
Swan waiting earnestly for a sour fish,
Lush trees beside the brook,

Giving the heritage site of view,
On my arrival,
Another catamaran arrives near me,
Offering me for a ride through the brook,
Gracefully I accept his offer,
The river water splashed on my hands,
Trees that lay beside me has camera,
That flashes the sunlight on me,
Making me glow in sunrays,
The voyage on the brook is gifted,
Since it has the tranquility,
The voyage made me to realize,
How blessed I am!
Till my eyes could see,
There's no abode.
But there's a tiny hut, emitting fragrance of culture,
As the catamaran touched the shores,
I stepped up and thanked the fisherman,
For giving the best ride of my life,
Nature's always rejuvenating and refreshing!
Absorb the beauty of brooks,
To zeal your life!

29. Rain

The cottons in the sky turning grey,
Cool breeze uplifting the ambience,
Flies flying all over the sky,
Trees longing to quench thirst,
Ponds, streams drying itself in thirst,
People looking over for the droplets,
It is the cluster of hope,
Sun reaching his hideout,
Is the masculine beauty of showers!
First pearl like droplet that falls off,
Brings wide smiles that went missing,
It secretes honey in farmer's heart,
Finally their prayer to Lord Indra is heard,
To have mercy on them!
Treading in showers without an umbrella,
Admiring the real elixir of nature,
In the beauty of wetness,
Is the feminine beauty of Rain!
Stream that ran dry and empty,
It is filled with competing waters,
They quenched their thirst.
If the first pearl is nourished,

Last pearl should be cherished too.
The essence of petrichor stands unbeaten.
It is the best moment after rainfall!
Petrichor mixing in the gentle wind,
Registers the birth of optimism!
Trees that drank abundant water,
Stored few for its future in its roots!
Ponds, streams rejuvenated,
Began to breathe again!
If golden cottons,
Is said to be the essence of optimism,
The greyish cottons,
Is the optimism of its own kind!
Rain brings life to Earth,
Doing several good things,
But expecting nothing back,
Rain adds a feather,
In the beautiful crown of nature!

30. Self Journey

Sauntering on the walking lane,
Alone in the early dawn of the day,
Admiring the elixir and lightness of sun,
In the hustle of gentle breeze,
The warmth of sun soothing the weariness,
Birds chirping to wake sleepy mankind,
Dew drops in the grass faking to be a pearl,
Spiritual centers getting cleansed,
Colorful rangoli welcoming colorful life,
Tiny kids carrying heavy baggage,
With these every day morning sights,
I kept wandering far away from my abode,
To step in the mystery land,
Where I'm the only person there,
My footprints are the first to be printed,
My eyes told me not to believe it,
I pinched myself, hard and harder,
To make sure that it's a reality,
I screamed in extreme agony,
My sense said it's a fantasy land,
Nature's beauty lies in front of me,
She stood with me,

Hand in hand, shoulder to shoulder,
Between the green fields lays a narrow path,
To the beautiful waterfalls,
I'm ever going to witness in my life,
The origin of the gorgeous beauty,
Seemed from the mountains of heaven,
It tastes the sweetest,
She slays her watery hair like the sword,
Piercing right into my heart,
But it never aches,
Little fishes tactfully blowing the cuts,
Besides this gorgeous there's another,
The stellar rose garden,
There are roses of all colors,
Black and brown, red and pink,
As I stepped into the valley of roses,
The petals which are so soft and light,
Bloomed in the ecstasy of life,
In meeting the beautiful girl,
Thorns shrugged its body to unharm me,
Tiniest birds playing over there,
Designed a beautiful crown,
And placed it on my head,
I bowed to the queen of gardens,
Before I made to the rare vegetation,
The vegetation isn't an ordinary kind,
It beholds the sweetest fruit,

The second that I bite it,
My soul healed.
I kept strolling to unveil,
The natural beauty to my eyes,
And serve it to my heart,
There's a life outside the city gates,
Which heals, soothes, rejuvenates,
The tiring weary souls,
Inherit those natural gifts,
To stop counting on pills,
Nature is the greatest healer,
Hence she is named as nature.

31. Exploring Lives

Life has many doors in it,
Each door has its uniqueness,
Opening each of the doors,
Unlocks the treasures of life,
Opening the door of happiness,
Gives you joy, ecstasy, bliss,
It makes you feel like flying,
Thank God for gifting you happiness,
Next day you might open the door,
That's full of sadness, mourning,
Don't curse or blame God,
Thank God for showing you worst,
You might unlock the door of success,
Enjoy the success with full heart,
But do remember to remain grounded,
Thank God for presenting you success,
You may open the door of failure,
Embrace the failure,
Since it's a good teacher,
Thank God for teaching you failure,
You might open the door of wrath,
Know how to control the destructive weapon,

Since it shatters everything,
Thank God for holding control of your wrath,
Opening the door of betrayal,
Destroys the good character in you,
Kill the thought of betrayal as it sprouts,
Thank God for killing your betrayal,
Unlocking the door of surprises,
Might push you to feel overwhelmed,
Have the feel but don't expect more,
Thank God for giving you surprises,
Unbolting the door of fear,
Can make you shiver, shattered and broken,
So break your fears before it breaks you,
Thank God for breaking your fears,
Unlatching the door of love,
Brings all smiles in your heart,
Spread love but love yourself first,
Thank God for loving you through love,
Opening the door of hatred,
Might break the bonds of relations,
Break the rock of hatred to pieces,
Thank God for helping you to break the hatred,
Unlock every door of your life,
To present yourself a new thing,
That makes your days colorful,
Explore life to its depth,
To see its real depth!

32. Time

Very few things in the world,

Are so precious and priceless,

One among such thing,

That is valuable is time,

Time never sees social statuses,

Time never distinguishes classes,

It is one and the same for all,

May be the day and night differs,

The clocks worldwide shows the same,

But some fast forward it,

By adjusting in clock,

Enjoy each second,

As you prosper yourself,

Time passes like the clouds quickly,

Compete with it to feel satisfied,

Mourning for the time lost,

It's a fool's act,

Preparing and managing the time,

Leads you to the way of success,

Working your time with smartness,

Compensates with the time that's lost,

It brings glory to the future,

Life and time are to be balanced,
Time builds cliff,
And the same time destroys empires,
Bad times teaches you,
The real face of the life,
Good times tells you,
About the flatterers of the life,
In every day of your life,
Have time for yourself,
That chases your dream!

33. Suicide

The man's act of cowardice,

It is committing suicide,

We aren't here in this earth,

All by ourselves, without any help,

God created us,

Our mother endured the agony,

For holding us in her arms, to give life,

She didn't beget us, love us and embrace us,

To see us motionless and lifeless,

Hanging in her saree,

And she witnessing it,

She dies thousands of deaths in that moment,

It's not the best gift you give her,

Impossible is a life without problem,

If for a problem,

One starts to think of suicide,

Humanity will vanish the next day,

Doctors are also humans like us,

They have plenty of life saving works,

Rushing a suicide attempt coward,

Into the wards pressures the doctors,

Taking pills, drowning in river,

Stabbing oneself, jumping in front of train,
Burning oneself, cutting the veins,
There are several ways to end a life,
But, learning to solve the problems,
Living the life to its fullest as God gifted us,
It is the best choice to choose,
If God gives a problem today,
Sometimes later, he will give the solution,
For that one must live on,
Burn the suicidal thoughts,
And let the life bloom.

34. Death

The thing that is born,
In this tiny bit of earth,
Has a fate with death,
In the very time of its creation,
Birth is cherished,
Death is inevitable,
Death of a creature,
Has another life in the world,
Death isn't the end,
But the new beginning!